To

Adrienne

We are on this journey because of your
help, encouragement, and belief in us...

www.mascotbooks.com

Rescuing Reed: The Little Dog Who Could

For more information, please contact:
Mascot Books
560 Herndon Parkway #120
Herndon, VA 20170
info@mascotbooks.com

Library of Congress Control Number: 2017911603

CPSIA Code: PBANG1017A
ISBN-13: 978-1-68401-395-1

Printed in the United States

Rescuing Reed

The Little Dog Who Could

Written by
Heidi Kristan Mottin

Illustrated by
Stephanie Fliss

Once
upon a time,
there was a little black pit bull
puppy who got lost on the streets of New York City. He was far away from his
mother and his brothers and sisters.

He didn't know what to do, so he followed friendly looking people walking by,
hoping they'd pick him up. He begged for food outside of restaurants and sat
nicely outside of hotels, but no one stopped to help the little black puppy.

So, he tried to be brave. He ate the food restaurants threw away in their alleys, and he drank out of puddles and leaky rainspouts.

But the little black puppy was sad and all alone.

A few days later, the dog catchers came through the streets. They saw the little black puppy and knew he was all by himself. They tried to catch him with their net, but the little black puppy was too quick.

Finally, the puppy got tired of running and the dog catchers snatched him up with their net and put him in their truck. They were headed to a place called Animal Control, a very scary place where dogs who have no homes are taken to live. That was the beginning of a long, hard road for the little black puppy.

For the next four years, he lived in a cement box all by himself. There were people called shelter workers who fed him and gave him water, but no one ever stopped to love him. He couldn't even stretch out his legs to play, because there was no room in the cement box. He wanted to explore and learn new things, but no one would teach him. Instead, he'd just sit and listen to the other dogs barking all day and all night.

But the one thing the shelter workers did give him was a name: *Reed*. Reed was a very sad puppy.

Over time, other dogs in the shelter went home with new families to happy lives, but no one ever came to see Reed. No one ever picked him to go home with their family.

So Reed kept sitting in his cement box, watching dogs leave for their new homes while new dogs from the animal catchers came and took their places. Dogs came and went, but Reed still sat there, all alone.

One sunny spring day, a lady named Heidi came to volunteer at the shelter. She started visiting Reed almost every day and even told him that he was the cutest little black dog she had ever seen. Reed was so surprised. No one had ever paid so much attention to him!

Heidi told Reed that she was going to help him be the best dog he could be. He was so excited that he jumped all over her and grabbed at her sleeves and pant legs. He could hardly wait!

First, Heidi taught Reed how to properly greet her when she came to visit. She told him that a big, jumping dog can be scary. He didn't scare her, but he needed to learn good manners or else he'd frighten everyone away.

This was harder than Reed thought! He was just so excited to see someone every day, he couldn't help it! He had a lot to learn.

But Reed was just as determined as Heidi, and before long, he learned how to come out of his cement box without jumping and grabbing at Heidi's clothes. So, she told him that they'd do new and fun things every day.

Reed couldn't wait!

Heidi played ball with Reed outside, taught him to sit, took him for long hikes, gave him baths, and cuddled with him in the grass.

Reed finally knew what it was like to be loved. But at the end of their visits, Heidi had to go home and Reed had to go back into his cement box. It was the worst part of Reed's day. He didn't like listening to all of the other homeless dogs cry, whimper, and bark.

One day, Heidi brought another little homeless dog outside to play with Reed. Her name was Patty. Reed was so excited, but he remembered his manners and the playdate went GREAT! He loved playing with Patty, and they soon became good friends and played together every day.

Since Reed was such a good boy playing with Patty, Heidi slowly introduced Reed to new playmates. Reed loved it and he quickly became one of the friendliest dogs at the shelter!

Reed was finally able to have a roommate in his cement box! A very pretty red pit bull dog named Jessie moved in with him, and they got to move into a bigger cement box! Reed loved his new roommate because they could play and snuggle together and they were never alone.

But one day, Jessie went to live in her forever home and once again, Reed was left by himself in the cement box. That night, Heidi came to visit him and told him she had a plan to make him a part of her family. She said it was not going to be easy, but she was determined to see it through.

The next day, Heidi brought her husband, Doug, to the shelter and they took Reed home. He could not believe it! He knew Heidi believed in him and that this was his special chance.

At first, Reed was a crazy guy in the house, running and running and running and bouncing around everywhere! Being in a home was SO new for him.

After a couple of months, Reed calmed down and settled into his new home. He learned that Heidi and Doug were his family and that made him the happiest dog in the world. But that wasn't all!

Heidi and Doug took Reed to training classes to teach him some tricks and how to behave like a good boy.

Eventually, Reed became such a good dog that he took some very hard tests and became a therapy dog. As a therapy dog, Reed is able to visit children in schools and hospitals to make them happy. The days that Reed visits with children are his favorite days.

And that is the story of how Reed turned into the little dog who could. All it took was one person to give him a chance, believe in him, and show him that he was worth something.

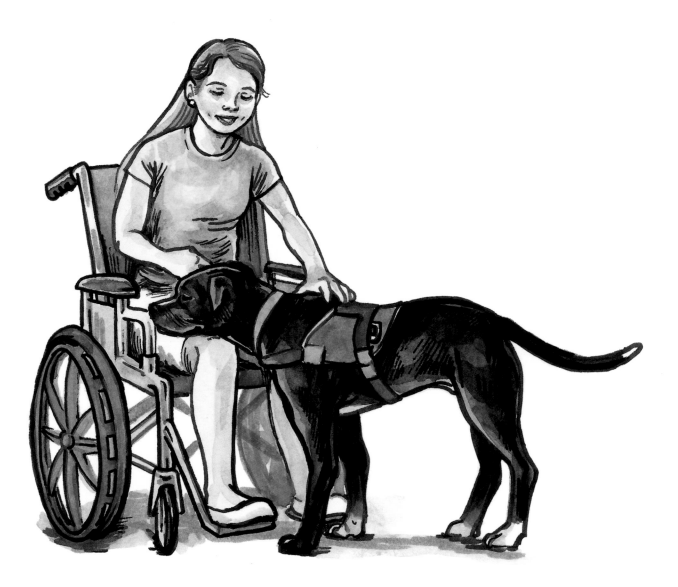

Reed went above and beyond everyone's wildest dreams, including his own. No one could have ever imagined that Reed would be a calm and loving dog, let alone a therapy dog for children. But he's doing just that, and he LOVES it!

Children, let Reed's story teach you something:

Don't ever let anyone tell you that you are not important and that you don't have a purpose. Please don't ever let anyone else feel that way either.

All it takes is one person. One person to believe in someone, one person to care about someone, one person to give someone a chance.

That can be all it takes for a person to finally believe in oneself and become the best person that they can be.

Heidi Kristan Mottin is an avid volunteer in animal shelters in southeastern Pennsylvania, where she works with pit bulls and other misunderstood breeds. She also has two rescued pit bulls of her own, Reed and Rooney.

Heidi and Reed work with students and sick children in hospitals as a therapy dog team, where Heidi shares Reed's triumphant tale with everyone. After seeing how much his story resonates so powerfully with all who hear it, she decided to publish the story in order to spread hope, encourage animal rescue, and bring about breed awareness.

Have a book idea?

Contact us at:

info@mascotbooks.com | www.mascotbooks.com